A STEP BY STEP B
ROTTW EILERS

HEINRICH VON BEINE

Title page: Rottweilers have become one of the most popular dog breeds available today. They have much to recommend them, as they are strong, intelligent, loyal, and great protectors of home and family. Photo by Robert Pearcy.

Distributed in the UNITED STATES by T.F.H. Publications, Inc., 211 West Sylvania Avenue, Neptune City, NJ 07753; in CANADA to the Pet Trade by H & L Pet Supplies Inc., 27 Kingston Crescent, Kitchener, Ontario N2B 2T6; Rolf C. Hagen Ltd., 3225 Sartelon Street, Montreal 382 Quebec; in CANADA to the Book Trade by Macmillan of Canada (A Division of Canada Publishing Corporation), 164 Commander Boulevard, Agincourt, Ontario M1S 3C7; in ENGLAND by T.F.H. Publications Limited, 4 Kier Park, Ascot, Berkshire SL5 7DS; in AUSTRALIA AND THE SOUTH PACIFIC by T.F.H. (Australia) Pty. Ltd., Box 149, Brookvale 2100 N.S.W., Australia; in NEW ZEALAND by Ross Haines & Son, Ltd., 18 Monmouth Street, Grey Lynn, Auckland 2 New Zealand; in SINGAPORE AND MALAYSIA by MPH Distributors (S) Pte., Ltd., 601 Sims Drive, #03/07/21, Singapore 1438; in the PHILIPPINES by Bio-Research, 5 Lippay Street, San Lorenzo Village, Makati Rizal; in SOUTH AFRICA by Multipet Pty. Ltd., 30 Turners Avenue, Durban 4001. Published by T.F.H. Publications Inc. Manufactured in the United States of America by T.F.H. Publications, Inc.

CONTENTS

HISTORY OF BREED

The Rottweiler, like all other domestic breeds, is the result of many years of selective breeding by devoted enthusiasts who were determined to retain and develop a working variety of dog that had existed in Germany for centuries. The root stock of the breed was to be found in the province of Swabia and especially in the region of Rottweil, the town from which the breed derives its name.

Rottweil, from the time of the Roman invasion of southern Europe, developed into a flourishing place of commerce. Cattle were driven many miles to be sold in its famous market, but such journeys were always hazardous. The drovers needed dogs that could keep the stock in check and defend them from man and beast. The very nature of the task was such that the dogs needed to be both large and, when required, decidedly unfriendly!

Within the town itself, there were many butchers who sold their meat both locally and in the neighboring villages, to which the meat was transported by small carts pulled by one or more dogs. Traders were subject to the same risks as the drovers, so their needs from the dogs were much the same. It is said that the butchers and drovers attached their money to their dog's collar as a safety precaution, their reasoning being that it was more difficult to rob the dog than the owner!

The breeding of the dogs would have been very informal, the main criteria being the dog's strength, ferocity, and size. Any that failed the demands of their role would be unlikely to live, let alone perpetuate their genes through matings. Those with reputations for their abilities would be much sought after, resulting in a concentration of their genes with those of similar

The Rottweiler is a large, robust, and powerful dog. His compact build denotes great strength, agility, and endurance. Photo by Isabelle Francais.

standing; this would create a degree of uniformity over a number of years. Size would have been within certain tolerances as the use of dogs in pairs, to pull carts, would encourage the establishment of size to weight compatibility. Color, like other beauty aspects, was of secondary importance, though black and brown were a preferred combination.

Certainly, with the passage of time, a breed of fixed type became associated with the butchers of Rottweil, and one is depicted on a guild sign in Rottenburg dating back to the eighteenth century. However, the very virtues of the breed were almost its undoing.

The Decline

As new towns began to appear in the area, so the influence of Rottweil started to wane. Long cattle drives became

Champion Pomác's Graf Tanzer, by American and Canadian Champion Graudstark's Pegasus, C.D., out of Champion Hallmark's "The Sting." Greg and Lori Benkiser, owners.

Young Majorhausen's Famous Pagan, C.D., poses with Champion Countess Cheska, C.D., T.D.X. Mrs. Minette Barlaug of Prince George, British Columbia, Canada, owns these handsome dogs.

less frequent and were ultimately outlawed; the number of butchers needing draft and guard dogs fell, and so did the number of dogs. The Napoleonic wars ravaged the area and the full effect of these various factors, together with the changing patterns of life created by the Industrial Revolution, resulted in there being just one bitch registered in Rottweil by 1905.

Breed Societies

Fortunately, the changing social structures had created a new type of dog owner—the middle class enthusiasts—who quickly organized themselves in order to both preserve and develop the former working breeds of their area. The problems they faced were considerable, for it must be remembered that the 'breeds' of the period were by no means definable by any present day standards. This resulted in differing opinions as to what constituted the desired type.

The first person to draft a standard for the breed was Albert Kull who, in 1901, produced a blueprint that embraced both the Rottweiler and the Leonberger. His original standard has been revised on numerous occasions, in order to be more precise in its wording and to take into account the very high degree of standardization that has been achieved over the years. Of course, the standard is now purely for the Rottweiler, the Leonberger being a totally separate breed with its own standard.

The first breed club to be formed was the Deutscher Rottweiler Klub (DRK), but only months after its inception in

Australia has produced some fine Rottweilers, among them Australian Champion Rotvel Trooper, Tarinbeck Camilla, and Australian Champion Rotvel Skyhigh—all distinguished winners of tremendous merit. Captain Craig Bryan, owner.

Heidelberg, 1907, a second club was created which was ultimately called the International Rottweiler Klub (IRK). Both maintained their own records, stud book, and objectives, which placed differing emphasis on the needs of the breed. The DRK felt that working qualities were paramount, whereas the IRK saw uniformity of structure as the essential need. This situation resulted in confusion that was made worse by the formation of a third club in 1919.

Happily, the DRK and the IRK patched up their differences and, in 1921, united to form the Algemeine Deutscher Rottweiler Klub (ADRK) which, to this day, remains the ruling body of the breed in Germany. The new club stabilized the breed's affairs, and in 1924 the third club joined to create a single administrative body.

The Spread of the Breed

With total control, the ADRK was able to address contentious aspects — such as the head shape — as well as introducing a breed warden system to monitor type and breeding potential of stock in any given area. The success of this system is evidenced both by the breed we have today and the high number of quality dogs exported annually from Germany.

Two world wars were to help spread the breed's reputation as a superb police and war dog, though outside of its homeland, it was overshadowed by its three fellow-country contemporaries: the German Shepherd Dog, the Boxer, and the

Rottweilers are excellent family protectors. Here Martyn Windeyer, nephew of Captain Craig Bryan of Australia, poses with his pal, Australian Champion Rotvel Skyhigh.

Doberman Pinscher. Each of these breeds made far greater progress between and after the wars. Although dogs were exported to the UK and the USA prior to 1940, it was not until the mid 1960's that the Rottweiler really started to generate interest, as is shown by the dramatic increase in registrations during and since that decade.

The Rottweiler Club of Great Britain was founded in 1960 and did much to foster interest in the breed, as do the various other regional clubs that have now emerged. Increased show entries, together with a growing number of dogs gaining working qualifications, both provided the breed with the opportunity to display its many abilities and stalwart character.

In the USA, an attempt was made in the 1940's to establish a national club, but this proved premature and it was not until the late 1950's that specialty clubs started to form. The three oldest are the Medallion, the Colonial, and the Golden Gate, while the national club, created in 1973, is the American Rottweiler Club.

The situation in Australia is a clear demonstration of the breed's changing fortunes. The first litter to be imported created interest but no buyers, resulting in all but one of the puppies being put down. This was in 1962. Just nine years later the first specialty club was formed in Victoria and was followed by further clubs in South Australia, NSW and, more recently, in Western Australia. To establish any breed in Australia is very difficult due to the extremely stiff quarantine regulations. Any dog imported, other than from New Zealand, must first spend both a period of quarantine and of residency in the UK before it can be imported into Australia, where it still has a period of quarantine to complete—a very expensive proposition for would-be importers of dogs. In spite of this, the Rottweiler has a very strong following in that country and a pool of stock is trying to meet the growing demand for the breed.

The story is the same in all other countries: wherever the Rottweiler goes, it keeps on winning new friends. The problems faced in establishing the breed around the world have now been replaced by just how to control the dramatic success the breed in enjoying. There is a growing market for companion guard dogs as well as for those used by enthusiasts for exhibition. More are being used for working trials, while the police, army, and security companies have all recognized the breed's great potential. It is inevitable that the Rottweiler is attracting a number of breeders whose only objective is to profit from the popularity of the breed, this following the same pattern seen with any "fashionable" breed.

It must be hoped that the qualities of character and usefulness, which are the hallmark of the Rottweiler, are nei-

A pair of four-month-old Rottie pups from the Ebshine Kennels in New South Wales, Australia. The breed has become quite popular in the land down under.

ther compromised nor sacrificed in order to meet superficial desires. Beginners are in a position to help the breed simply by being very selective in both the quality of puppies they buy and from where they buy them. It is hoped that within this publication will be found pointers that will be helpful when purchasing, as well as sound advice on just how to look after one's first Rottweiler.

CHOICE AND CARE

The decision to acquire a Rottweiler should not be made until the whole family has been consulted. Only if this is to everyone's agreement should matters proceed further. Which is preferred, a male or a female? A puppy or an adult? Is the dog required purely as a companion or is there interest in exhibiting or even breeding? These aspects decided, one can then search for a suitable source from which the puppy can be purchased. If each question is carefully considered, then the chances of later disappointment will be greatly reduced and many years of happy Rottweiler ownership will be assured.

Two-way Suitability

It should never be assumed that any breed of dog is suited to all people, nor they to a given breed. This is especially true in relation to the working breeds, and particularly so with those dogs associated with guard work. The very nature of the latter means that such breeds must possess a strong protective instinct, coupled with the power to make their presence felt. These qualities are hallmarks of the Rottweiler and, as such, make them unsuitable for a great many households. Elderly people would find the breed very difficult to control. Those who live alone and go out to work are not recommended to keep any dog, as this is unfair to the animal which is very social in its needs.

If one has not owned dogs before, then the Rottweiler cannot be recommended as one would be better advised to choose a breed with a more placid temperament than trying to cope with the somewhat fiery disposition of the Rottweiler.

Before acquiring a Rottweiler, make certain this is the breed for you. These powerful, muscular dogs are not necessarily suitable for everyone or for every lifestyle. Photo by the late Alton Anderson.

This breed is more suited to those with previous experience either with guard breeds, large breeds, or those, such as Bull Terriers, which need firm handling and discipline.

Rottweilers are very muscular dogs beyond which, like any animal, they vary in their attitude toward children (often reflecting the way they have been socialized as puppies). Some are very benign; others are less tolerant to being pulled about by young children. This is a fact of life and it would be irresponsible of parents if they did not seriously ponder this point. A nip from a Chihuahua is one thing, but the same from a Rottweiler is a totally different matter. Rottweilers are not a dangerous breed in the right hands, but they very much have that potential in the wrong home. This must be fully appreciated from the outset.

Dog or Bitch

With so many anti-mate products available today, including a canine "pill," the past problems associated with an in-season bitch are far less a factor than they were. Even so, the oestrum period of a female does entail some inconvenience for the owner and must be considered. A bitch can be spayed if it

Both male and female Rottweilers make fine companions. With regard to size, the former usually range between 24 and 27 inches in height, the latter 22 to 25 inches.

Choice and Care

Rottweiler puppies are not only cute and cuddly, but they are easy to train. Generally speaking, a young dog has not had time to develop bad habits. Donna M. Wormser of Ocala, Florida, bred this adorable seven-week-old pup.

is decided that one does not wish to breed and, contrary to old stories, there is no advantage to the bitch if she has "just one litter first."

A bitch is smaller than a dog, will eat less, and is less inclined to want to dominate her immediate family (and other dogs) as will a male. These are general rules but there is always that bitch who is not aware of the rules, so no trait should be considered as exclusive to either sex. Dogs are more disposed to fighting — usually their own sex — in order to constantly assert their authority. Unless they are kept in check, this can spill over into the family, where they become unruly. Far more dogs have to be found new homes on this account than do bitches.

Because of this desire "to be in charge," a dog will often prove more difficult to train, it being a test of wills between owner and the dog. In many households the day-to-day management of the family pet is very much the domain of the housewife and, with this in mind, the bitch is possibly the better choice.

It is difficult to determine if a six-week-old Rottweiler puppy has what it takes to be a champion in the show ring. Most breeders wait until their puppies have matured before predicting, with any certainty, a dog's show potential.

A male Rottweiler looks "more" of a Rottweiler than does a bitch and, together with its "tough guy" image, appeals more to men. However, this is a very poor reason to determine choice of sex. Bitches are generally cleaner in their personal habits and do not have the strong desire of the male to constantly leave their "mark" on everything from a tree to a store front or car hubcap!

Should you already own another breed, then choose the opposite sex in the Rottweiler (unless you plan to breed) as opposite sexes are *less* likely to fight each other. It should be added that, while bitches are more benign by nature, this does not mean they are any less protective of their home and family. When bitches do fight, they can be really mean, probably more so than dogs!

Choice and Care

Puppy or Adult

Clearly, in most cases, the puppy is the better choice, especially when it is required as a companion. It will have acquired no bad habits and can be molded into the family life more easily. You miss out on a great deal of fun if you opt for an adult. However, the family circumstances might dictate that a young adult is preferable, it having passed its formative stages and been house-trained and so on. Maybe you wish to give an adult that had previously been mistreated a better home? This is a fine thought, but caution should be exercised as it is most likely such a Rottweiler will need very experienced handling in order that it be re-socialized. It is sure to be delinquent to a greater or lesser degree and you will not know to what extent until you actually own it.

A young adult may well be the choice of potential breeder/exhibitors. The important development period of the puppy's life will have been accomplished under the eye of an experienced breeder and the dog's potential will be more easily seen. It may also have been exhibited and gained experience in

Check with your local pet shop for toys that are safe and durable; avoid those that could easily break into small chunks and be swallowed by your dog.

the show ring; maybe it has even brought home some wins. The price for such a dog, however, will be quite a bit higher than for a puppy. Again, caution will need to be exercised as to how the puppy has been socialized to family life. It may have been totally different from the home into which it might be going.

Breeding Potential

For those wanting to breed, and maybe do some exhibiting as well, the bitch is the better proposition. If a young male fails to achieve its early potential, then its future use as a stud dog, in a one dog family, is virtually nil. There are just too many top class winners to be had by those wanting to have their bitches covered. However, a bitch who had not made the hoped-for level in exhibition may well still be a potentially very sound brood bitch on which one can commence building a breeding program. Not every puppy must be a potential champion to be saleable.

Family Companion

Even if the family only wants a companion dog, they are still advised to follow a sound purchasing procedure. Obviously, even the most successful of breeders have those puppies that will not, for one reason or another, reach the standard required for exhibiting or breeding; the pup might be slightly mismarked, have less than ideal dentition, or a similar show fault. These matters will not affect the puppy's worth as a pet and, further, the pup will still have the same quality of breeding behind it that its more illustrious littermates have. The character of such a pup is potentially every bit as good as any champion (and might even be better!) so they make wonderful companions and are usually available at reasonable prices. Bear in mind that no Rottweiler will ever be cheap, even a pet-quality one.

Cost of Upkeep

The initial cost of a Rottweiler, high though it may appear, is nothing compared to what it will cost to keep during its lifetime. All too often one sees owners who have purchased large breeds only to then find they are unable to afford their

upkeep. The Rottweiler is a large dog and enjoys a very healthy appetite. If you have to ponder the food cost and possible veterinarian fees that might come along, then chances are you cannot afford this breed. Other costs will be higher too, such as collars and leads, bedding, dog crates, and items such as boarding fees, should these ever be applicable. Nothing is worse than seeing an underfed dog whose owners clearly did not take ongoing costs into their initial considerations.

Showing off his working ability is American and Canadian Champion Daverick's Alex vom Hasenkamp, C.D., who pulled eight-month-old Anne Rogers Gordon two miles in a local Halloween parade. Alex and Anne received much applause throughout the entire event and brought home first prize in the "Tiny Tots" division! The Richard Gordons, Moorestown, New Jersey, owners.

Purchasing Procedures

Assuming, all factors considered, you are satisfied that you can cope with the demands of a Rottweiler, then the next stage toward purchasing one is to see as many examples of the breed as you can. The very worst way to buy a puppy is to glance at your local newspaper and rush out to buy from a litter purely because it is convenient or available at that moment. Buy in haste; repent at leisure!

The beginner is strongly advised to make contact with a local pet shop, who will inform them both of breeders in their area and of the nearest Rottweiler Club. They may also be able to advise when and where the next Rottweiler, or all-breeds show is to be seen. A dog show is a good starting point as many of the top breeders will be there exhibiting and will give one the opportunity to see many fine examples of the breed. Shows are advertised in various newspapers. If you are interested in the working side of the breed, then you should seek out those who specialize in this, and whose breeding lines have a proven record of having strong working abilities.

Hip Status

All heavy-boned breeds are susceptible to hip dysplasia, a malformation of the hip joint. The best safeguard you can obtain in respect to this is to only consider a puppy whose sire *and* dam have been X-rayed for their hips and who have gained a satisfactory score. Most countries have schemes in operation for evaluating hips and your veterinarian or breed club will advise you on this. To purchase a puppy from un–X-rayed stock is to take quite unnecessary risks.

This youngster, from the Beenen "A" litter, doesn't seem to enjoy being confined to his pen. Lin and Don Beenen of Lowell, Michigan, breeders.

The greatest physical problem seen in Rottweilers is hip dysplasia, although other large, heavily-boned breeds suffer from this malformation of the hip joints as well. When you purchase a Rottweiler, make certain that its hips have been certified normal by the Orthopedic Foundation for Animals (OFA).

Visiting Kennels

Provided you have done your homework on the status of various breeders, then there will be little risk of your being sold a poor puppy. Good kennels and pet shops will be clean, with no dirty water dishes or bowls of uneaten food lying around. Above all, the stock should look well cared for and obviously happy. A breeder who is more anxious to sell you a puppy than to find out if you are a suitable owner is a breeder to avoid.

Be sure you are prompt once an appointment is made

and only handle puppies when invited to. A healthy puppy is self-evident and will be lively and plump (but not pot-bellied). Its eyes will be clear and free from any signs of discharge. The nose will be moist but not wet, and its breath will have a clean, fresh puppy smell. The paws and joints may seem oversized, but this is quite normal in all large breeds. The puppy should stand and run about without any difficulty or abnormality. The skin should be glossy, and, if brushed against its lie, should exhibit no signs of fleas or other parasites at the base of the hairs. The skin will be loose, but not excessively so.

Any puppy that hides away in a corner is either ill or will need very special handling so is not recommended; but having gone to a breeder of repute, it is very unlikely you will see such a pup.

A few breeders conduct aptitude tests on their puppies in order to try to match pup with owner. This is very much in its infancy at this time but, *correctly* done, has much to recommend it. Essentially, the object is to place the bold, out-going pup with a similar person. The more subdued youngster is placed with an owner whose personality is likewise and to whom the puppy will react more favorably than to an over-zealous person.

Good breeders will be very open with you as to the merits of their stock. As they will have no problems in selling it they, therefore, have nothing to gain from trying to be other than totally honest. Once a puppy has been chosen, you are advised to pay a deposit if the puppy is to be collected on another date. This confirms your intent.

Age

Although most puppies are eight to ten weeks old when they go to their new homes, there has been much research into the ideal age for such a move and it clearly suggests that seven weeks is the ideal. At such an age it can adjust far more easily to new situations and sounds (vacuum cleaners, washing machines, and so on). Much after seven weeks and any adverse stress can result in imprintings which will be life-long, though not unduly apparent at the time to the untrained eye. All of this would suggest that prospective Rottweiler own-

ers will need to begin their plans to purchase many weeks *before the puppy is even born.*

Worming and Vaccinations

Puppies are normally wormed at two weeks of age and repeat doses are given every three weeks to the age of six months; thereafter twice yearly. *Toxocara canis* is the most

This impressive dog, American and Canadian Champion Rodsden's Kato v Donnaj, C.D.X., T.D., was the first Rottweiler to win Best in Show in the United States. Jan Marshall of Donnaj Kennels in Woodstock, Vermont, handled Kato to all of his wins.

common roundworm while *Dipylidium* sp. are the tapeworms most likely to be seen. Heartworm is also a potential hazard. Your veterinarian should be consulted for treatment of each of these parasites.

The major diseases against which puppies need protection are distemper, canine hepatitis, leptospirosis, and parvovirus. Vaccines are normally given in a combined form, at eight weeks and twelve weeks, with boosters at varying intervals thereafter. Owners should check with their veterinarian over the vaccines as treatment may vary depending on the vac-

cine manufacturer. If the puppy has already received its first injection when it is purchased, then the breeder will supply the appropriate certificate which should be shown to your vet.

Paperwork

As well as the vaccination certificate, the breeder will normally supply you with the following papers:

1. *Pedigree*   This is usually of four or five generations and will indicate which of the puppy's ancestors have gained show or working titles both in your country or elsewhere. Often it will also indicate the registration numbers of the forebears, which can be most useful should you wish to do research into particular dogs cited.

There is nothing cuter than a litter of Rottweiler pups, as they look like little teddy bears! These youngsters enjoy the company of Bonnie Wimberly of Delphi Rottweilers.

2. *Registration Document*   It is very probable that the litter of puppies will have been registered by the breeder with their kennel club. The puppies may even have been individually named and registered, though this is unlikely with pups

Breeders often classify their puppies as show- breeder- or pet-quality Rottweilers. Naturally, those dogs with superior show potential or the ability to produce champion offspring will be more expensive than household pets. Many breeders, however, are not concerned so much with beauty and show conformation as they are with working ability and achievements in obedience competition. Photo by Ron Reagan.

sold as pets. The breeder will supply the documents applicable, together with a transfer form in order that the new owner be able to transfer the dog or bitch to their own name. Without correct documentation the new owner will not be able to exhibit his/her Rottweiler.

Usually kennel clubs are slow in issuing registrations. This might mean that these papers will be sent on to you when they are received by the breeder. Registration procedure varies from one club to another, so the foregoing is a general guide. The new owner should contact the national controlling club or association for applicable regulations.

3. *Diet Sheet*   This will show the breeder's feeding regimen. It should be continued for at least three weeks in order that the puppy has fully adjusted to its new home before its diet is changed.

Preparing for the Puppy

It is advisable to purchase a number of items that the puppy will need in advance of the pup's homecoming. Food and water dishes of aluminum or stoneware are preferred to those made of plastic. Plastic will not last long with a Rottweiler pup.

A dog crate is an expensive but worthwhile investment. These can be used as the puppy's sleeping quarters but also double as carry crates when you wish to take your dog with you, yet wish to be able to contain it (in a hotel, for example). The puppy will soon come to regard this as its own special place to which it can retire when it does not wish to be disturbed. This privacy must be respected by children. You will need a large size crate for a Rottweiler.

Should you not purchase a crate from the outset, then a stiff cardboard box is a good idea for the puppy's first bed. The pup will chew at this and it is easily replaced, whereas a basket receiving similar treatment is expensive. Once the puppy passes its teething stage it is time to purchase a more suitable bed. Whether crate or box, the bed should be lined with old

Windwalker Kennels of Port Crane, New York, own this three-month-old puppy, Von Bruka Jaguar.

If bred, trained, and handled properly, a Rottweiler puppy will mature to be one of the finest protection dogs and family companions you could ever own.

blankets so it is nice and snug.

Puppy playpens can be purchased or made by the handy person. They can be useful for containing the pup when you are not able to watch over it. It can be placed in the garden (yard) on nice days, but not for long periods, especially when it is very sunny, as the pup cannot then avoid the sunlight if it so desires.

A suitable comb and brush will be needed together with a puppy collar and lead. Any playthings purchased should be of very durable manufacture if they are to survive the attention of a Rottweiler puppy. Nylabone® (hard, flavored nylon chews) and Gumabone® and Gumaball® products (which are hard, flexible toys) are very good. Squeaky plastic toys and similar flimsy products are not recommended as they will soon be torn apart and could be swallowed by the pup, with potentially fatal results.

A small stock of food as used by the breeder should be on hand together with any vitamin supplements that might have been recommended by the puppy's breeder. Buy your supplies from a quality pet store; the quality at most supermarkets is shockingly poor and relatively expensive.

Arrival Day

The puppy should be collected in the morning rather than late in the day, as this gives it more time to settle in on its first day in its new home. You are advised to transport the pup in a cardboard box, well-lined with old paper on top of old toweling. The pup might be sick on this journey, as it will take a few trips in the car before its body becomes accustomed to the sensation of movement. Long journeys should be broken with rest periods, preferably away from urbanizations or where other dogs may have been, so it won't pick up parasites. Once in its new home, the puppy should be offered a drink of luke-warm milk and then allowed to explore its immediate surroundings. If it is your intention to restrict the pup to certain rooms, then this should be observed from the outset. The puppy will want to sleep quite a bit and at such times it should not be disturbed. Young children *must* be taught that the puppy's rest periods are important to it. After a day or two it is wise to have your vet give the puppy a check-up, just to see that all is well. If you have any complaints about your pup's health, back it up with a vet's report.

The puppy's bed should be sited in a quiet, draft-free location. Young animals are notorious nibblers on anything that is new to them. With this in mind you should ensure there are no loose wires within reach. Beware of children or sudden gusts of wind slamming doors in which the puppy might get trapped, with very painful results.

Another common source of danger to both pet and human alike is when pups are running free in the kitchen while Mom is cooking the day's meal. It is so easy to forget the pup for a moment when handling boiling pans of food and then trip over the puppy! This is where the dog crate comes in real handy. The pup can watch what is going on without risk to itself and others.

Finally, check on the security of the yard gate. Self-closing types are best just in case someone forgets to close the gate behind them. See there are no holes in the fence through which the pup might escape unnoticed. Be sure garden ponds are also safe from an inquisitive puppy who might fall in.

Socialization of Rottweiler puppies is very important in order to bring out the best personality traits of this breed.

Sadly, all too often, one sees people who have a totally irresponsible attitude to the animals in their care to the degree that one is left wondering why they bothered to have them in the first place. The beginner should ponder a few of the obvious points that will ensure they do not become such people!

MANAGEMENT

At all times your Rottweiler should be under your control and *never* allowed to become a nuisance to neighbors. Nothing is worse than to live next door to an owner whose dog howls, whines, or barks day and night. Likewise, no one will appreciate your dog fouling the sidewalk, chasing their cats, digging up their flower beds, or even playfully jumping up at them with dirty paws. All of these are indicative of inconsiderate and, frankly, very bad dog owners.

A dog is like a child; it will only become unruly if it is allowed to be. Often, owners will say "This dog I can do nothing with," as though they had acquired some sort of canine idiot rather than admit they just had no idea of how to cope with a dog, nor had they — in truth — made any real efforts to do so. Anti-dog laws have *only* been introduced because of irresponsible owners creating a situation that society-at-large rejects.

Even normally well-cared-for and obedient dogs can create bad feeling if their owners allow them to foul public places such as parks, beaches, or country pathways. If you are not prepared to take responsibility for such occurrences then simply do not become a dog owner. Take with you one of the commercial "pooper-scoopers," paper and a plastic container. If this does not appeal to you then ensure that the dog fouls

According to the breed standard, the Rottweiler should exemplify sturdiness, stoutness, and substance without being fat or overpowering. Photo by Isabelle Francais.

your property before being taken onto public properties.

When out for the day with your dog always beware of unintentional cruelty to your pet. For example, you have left the dog in the car while you go to a shop. You get talking to a friend and forget the heat of the day and the fact that you closed all of the windows. So the poor dog slowly suffocates or suffers a heat-stroke.

Do not take your dog with you into busy shopping areas until it has become familiar being surrounded by many people, and to the hustle and bustle of city centers. Likewise, most

Although the Rottweiler is a working breed, some Rottie owners claim that their dogs can keep up with the best of the retrieving breeds! This pup is owned by Edith Alphin of Altar Kennels, Fayetteville, North Carolina.

dogs are frightened of firecrackers, gunshots, and door-slams; some dogs are even nervous of thunder and lightning and at such times might prefer a well-lit room (if it is nighttime).

Training Classes

Owners are strongly recommended to join in one of the area dog training classes, especially if their knowledge of training techniques is limited. At such places *you* will be taught how to teach your dog, the dog will learn its basic obedience, it will be gaining excellent experience at socializing with other dogs and people and, finally, the owner will enjoy the company of those with similar interests in dogs. Training a dog as independent as a Rottweiler really is a must, and at such classes you will be sure of getting the right advice. You will usually have an experienced trainer to help you over any difficult periods you may encounter with your dog. However, a word of warning! *There are many "cowboy" trainers who set themselves up as being experienced when quite the opposite is true.* Try to join a club where the credentials of the trainers are recommended to you by those whose knowledge you respect. Usually your local vet or pet shop can be helpful in selecting a training school.

House Training

A healthy puppy will normally defecate about six times a day and urinate even more frequently. The beginner should always remember that a puppy, unlike a young adult, has no

Champion Riegele's Astro von Eken at play with his favorite tire. Ellen B. Walls of Hartly, Delaware, owner.

voluntary control over its bowel movements and does it as it must. Therefore, be prepared and try to anticipate defecation. Shortly after feeding times, just after it has awakened from sleep, and after periods of play are prime times. Initially, a dirtbox layered with old newspaper on which some soil has been placed will suffice. Place the puppy in this at prime times. It will jump out at first but as soon as you see it preparing to defecate, quickly place it into the box. It will soon get the message. The box must be cleaned after each use — dogs are no different from humans in only wanting to use a clean toilet!

Obviously, an owner must be prepared to contend with a few puddles in the early days, but within a short time the pup will always go to its dirtbox. If it is taken into the yard first thing in the morning, and last thing at night, then its use of the dirtbox will become less frequent and it will eventually learn to control its bowels pending its daily exercise. It should be encouraged to use the same area of the yard for its toilet needs and in this way you will be able to either dig its feces into the earth or remove and burn them.

Owners without yards must rely on newspaper training.

Basic Training

The first commands any dog must learn are those of *heal, sit* and *stay* — together with that of *no*. Never bore a puppy with long sessions. Keep them short and always give lavish praise when a command is completed. This will produce far better results than if one is continually using negative terms. The tone of the voice is a trainer's prime tool. The use of force is a very poor method of training any animal. Teaching should be a gradual and on-going process, not something done once a week at the local club, or when the dog has done something wrong. This said, do not commence a training session when you are feeling "grumpy," as chances are you will soon be scolding the dog without just cause.

Teaching a puppy to *sit* is simply a case of pressing its hindquarters gently but firmly down, and saying the command at the same time. The *stay* follows on from the *sit*; once the latter is well understood then simply say *"stay"* and move back-

Champion Alec von Beenen, pictured at three months, was bred by Lin and Don Beenen and is owned by Dr. and Mrs. Royal Poel. Three months is about the right age to start basic obedience training, which is a must for Rottweilers if they are to become well-behaved canine citizens.

wards a step or two. The pup will start to follow you but should be returned to its original position and the routine repeated. Always remember that a dog wants nothing more than to please you so that any training failings are more likely to be your failure to communicate than the dog's to learn.

Lead training can commence as soon as the puppy has settled into its new home. At first, simply place the collar on the pup for short periods while you are playing with it. This way the puppy will soon get used to it. Next, attach the lead and let the puppy become accustomed to the restraint this creates. On no account should you drag the puppy around — as one often sees with people using what is essentially brute force methods. By coaxing or tempting the pup to follow you with the use of tidbits, you will obtain much better results.

Lead training should be done in the privacy of your home or yard. Public places present stress for the pup, as well as distraction from the job at hand. If you are able to train the puppy against a fence, then this is better as it restricts the puppy's lateral movement and it must then walk between the fence and your left leg; thus there is less need for you to pull the puppy about.

If the puppy begins to pull ahead of you, give the lead a short tug and say *"heel."* Remember: a short tug and not such that it causes pain to the puppy.

Choke chains are used by many people to collar train, but I have never considered these to be any more effective than a normal collar. Most stubborn dogs seem quite capable of pulling, even though they are clearly being half throttled into the process! It is altogether better that the dog responds to your voice than to choke action.

It is possible to purchase a *head-halter* similar to those used for horses but without a bit. Instead, a slip ring under the dog's jaw is used to attach the lead to. By gently raising one's arm, the noseband tightens, closing the dog's mouth and pulling the head toward the owner. Done correctly, the dog experiences no discomfort and certainly the owner has far more control over the dog than with more conventional chokes or collars. However, used badly, these are potentially more dangerous than chokes, so beginners are advised to seek correct instruction on their use.

Whenever the puppy does something it should not, then simply be firm in your command *"no"* and look the puppy straight in the eyes as you say it. Dogs are very sensitive to both the voice and the eye — both of which, together with complex facial gestures, are extensively used by wild dogs to communicate with each other. From these basic commands all other training can be developed because you will, by now, have established a rapport with your dog.

Finally, there is no time limit to basic training. Just because someone else's dog appears to be at a more advanced stage with his or her pup, has no meaning to yours. Rottweilers are slow to mature, they are not as easily trained as German Shepherd Dogs, and you are not in a race. Let the dog come along at its own pace and, in any case, you should not attempt any form of advanced training until the pup is at least eight or nine months old. Just be sure it has fully mastered its basics first.

Grooming Your Rottweiler

The Rottweiler needs no trimming and no heavy

grooming. However, grooming should be done on a regular basis, as in this way the coat will remain healthy. In the grooming process the owner can be on the lookout for any unwanted lodgers, such as lice or fleas. If the dog is groomed each week with a medium grade comb and then given a brisk brushing and a final polish with a chamois leather, its coat will always look glossy.

At this time, the ears, teeth, and nails can also receive routine checking. The ears should only need wiping inside with a cotton swab. Any build-up of dirt deep in the ear should be referred to a veterinarian. The teeth, given correct feeding and Nylabone® chew toys, should remain clean. With age, a build-up of tartar may occur, but this is easily removed by scaling the teeth. Your vet will attend to this for you, but he has to anesthetize your dog to do it. Start your puppy out with a Nylabone® and you might never have teeth trouble.

If a dog is exercised on hard ground, his nails will remain short; but if they do grow too long, then they may be clipped with guillotine-type clippers or filed. Care should be taken not to cut the quick. As this is difficult to see in dark nails, trim off only the tips, or let your vet or an experienced person do this for you.

Lice and fleas will be seen as gray or red parasites in the fur, usually at the base of the tail or behind the ears. Their droppings are seen as black specks when combed hair is held against a white background. In order to eradicate these parasites, it will be necessary to treat both the dog and its bedding. Repeat treatments will be required in order to kill unhatched eggs. As the flea is the intermediate host for the tapeworm,

Since Rottweilers have short, smooth coats, grooming them will be a cinch. This youngster is owned by Glenn Goreski of Dschungel Rottweilers, Wallington, New Jersey.

treatment for the latter is also advised. Your vet will prescribe a course of treatment. In hot weather, secondary infections created by the dog's scratching fleas can become a bigger problem than the parasites. Always check your dog's skin for any signs of swelling or reddish areas and consult your vet immediately if these are seen.

Entropion and Trichiasis in Rottweilers

These conditions are thought to be hereditary in their mode of transmission. Happily they are not as widespread in the Rottweiler breed as they once were. An *entropion* eyelid is one in which the outer edge turns in toward the eye, while *trichiasis* is where the eyelash turns in; both cause the dog considerable discomfort, made worse by the dog's continual rubbing of the eye with its paw.

Should your puppy exhibit obvious signs of an eye problem, the veterinarian should be consulted for advice. The condition might clear in a young puppy as its head develops; if not, an operation or two will effect a complete cure. From experience, should you be unfortunate to have a dog with this problem, then two operations are recommended. This way your vet need remove only a small amount of skin and then make adjustments on the second. If too much skin is removed in one operation, the dog can have an obvious "operated" look around the eye.

Rottweilers have become popular as guard dogs, protecting home, family, and property. These three sentinels are owned by Peter and Marilyn Piusz of Johnstown, New York.

Management

Left: Rottweilers have been used very successfully in police work. Here Sir Butkus Baby Bull, known as "Titan," poses with his owner, Sheriff Jay Sheffield. *Right*: The line-up at Welkerhaus Rottweilers, which belong to Rita Welker.

Exercise

The Rottweiler, like many other heavy, large-boned breeds, does not mature until it is about two years old, sometimes even older. It is essential that it is not over-exercised during this growing period as this can result in lifelong problems. If undue stress, through overplay, excessively rough play (especially jumping) is permitted, there is a very real probability that the pup will go lame on its front legs. Such stress on the joints and muscles will also affect rear movement. At the first signs of limping, the puppy's exercise must be restricted; it should be walked on a lead, not allowed to run after balls and other dogs. Of course, veterinary advice should be sought without delay. In Rottweilers, overweight accounts for many cases of lameness. Overweight coupled with over-exercise places great pressure on the developing bones, most of which are still being ossified during the early life of the dog. *"Everything in moderation"* must be the rule.

The feeding of dogs is essentially the application of common sense and observation of a basic knowledge of nutritional needs. Breeders vary greatly in their thoughts on this subject, and much has been written about it, so the beginner is advised to follow the feeding regimen of their puppy's breeder until such time that their own thoughts on the subject have been formed.

FEEDING

Dogs are primarily carnivores. They are adapted for flesh-eating. This does *not* mean they can subsist in a fully healthy condition on a totally all-meat diet. Indeed, no carnivore is exclusively a meat-eater, as all are, to a greater or lesser degree, omnivorous in their feeding habits. In the wild, wolves and dogs will eat berries, nuts, shoots, and certain plants when times get really hard. Normally, their vegetable needs are provided, partly digested, within the intestines of the animals on which they prey, all of which is eaten.

Constituents of Food

Apart from water, food is comprised predominantly of proteins, minerals, carbohydrates, and fats. Each of these fulfills a specific function in the body. Protein is needed in a puppy for healthy growth, so a pup's protein requirements are higher than those of an adult. Certain constituents of protein, known as amino acids, are vital and cannot be synthesized by the body so must be present in the diet. Protein of animal origin is richer in amino acids than is plant protein. Carbohydrates, such as found in dog meal and biscuits, are made from cereals and are a prime source of energy, while fats serve as concentrated energy and can be stored in body tissue for conversion to energy as required. Fats also make foods more palatable. Minerals are necessary for bone and tooth formation.

Dogs also require a minimum of thirteen vitamins which fulfill diverse roles ranging from assisting in the breakdown of foodstuffs to ensuring healthy eyesight. Minerals com-

Nylabone® is the safest therapeutic chewing device you can give your Rottweiler. It comes in various sizes, shapes, and flavors to suit any dog's taste. Just check with your local pet shop or with your veterinarian about these effective chew products.

prise the other major group of chemicals which must be present in the diet. In the case of a puppy, calcium and phosphorous are most important for they, along with vitamin D, are crucial to the development of healthy bone. The needed ratio of these to each other is specific, and excessive use of calcium supplements can upset this ratio with negative results. Calcium, for example, can be deposited in other tissues and this sets off a chain reaction resulting in metabolic imbalances. Other minerals, known as trace elements, are also needed and examples of these are zinc, iodine, copper, and manganese.

Types of Diet

There are basically three ways in which a dog may be fed. These are: a natural diet, one using canned foods, and one using dried or frozen foods.

Natural Diet Here one would feed fresh meat (cooked or raw) and supplement this with biscuit meal and vegetables. Concentrated vitamin supplements might also be given. This is the least convenient way to feed a dog and it carries with it the risk that a vital vitamin or mineral might be deficient in the diet, as these chemicals are often destroyed by cooking. Conversely, dogs have been fed in this way throughout recorded history and many will argue that such feeding regimens provide psychological as well as nutritional satisfaction. Certainly, the mastication needed to tear and consume raw meat does provide far better jaw muscle and teeth exercise than in diets where the dog's teeth are hardly needed, essentially based around pre-cooked and somewhat soft food.

If vitamin supplements are to be given, they should be given only under veterinary supervision, and to achieve a specific purpose. It is quite pointless trying to fill a dog up with such chemicals on the basis that if one gives enough of them then there will be no deficiencies. It just does not work that way. Although meat specifically for animal consumption can be purchased, the beginner is advised to buy only top choice butchers' meat; the same applies when buying chicken or fish. Horse meat is an acceptable food for dogs.

Canned Foods These are not only convenient but are also produced to a very high standard of content, fortified with the correct balance of vitamins and minerals. Clearly, some brands have a higher meat content than others (the cheaper ones containing more cereal), so one is better advised to choose a variety that appears "meaty" and which the dog obviously enjoys.

Dried and Frozen Foods Like canned foods, these are convenient, and in the case of dried foods, they are also very handy if you are travelling with your dog, as they are not at all messy. Dry foods must always be accompanied by water, but water should *always* be available to your dog anyway. Frozen foods must be thawed out completely before being fed, so

A complete, nutritionally-balanced diet will help keep your Rottweiler healthy and strong. If you prefer to prepare your own home-cooked meals, first check with your veterinarian to see that what you are offering your dog is correct for his size and age.

are less "instant" than canned or dried food.

Many owners take the middle road of feeding their dogs by utilizing each of the three ways described. This helps prevent a dog from becoming "finicky" over its food. Indeed, most dogs are great lovers of anything that even resembles food and are therefore prone to obesity.

Meal and Biscuit   These are available in various sizes, depending on the size of your dog. Biscuits are not a substitute for meat and should be regarded as a tidbit or snack. Both dog meal and biscuits are better if made from whole grain cereals. A suitable alternative, and one which adds variety to the diet, is to feed cooked rice in place of the cereal. In many countries rice is the staple diet for humans, dogs, and cats.

Amount of Food

The quantity of food needed, per day, by a dog will depend on numerous factors. A male dog, being larger, will normally require more than a bitch. Well-exercised Rottweilers will need more than those which do little, and older pets will need less than when they were in their prime. Dogs also differ, one to the other, in their make-up and this will also affect what each will need to maintain good condition. Climate will influence food intake. It requires more to keep a dog in cold climates than in hot ones. Finally, dogs recovering from illness, as well as in-whelp and lactating bitches, will also need more than their normal rations.

Because of these various factors, and their interaction, one cannot state that a given puppy needs a given amount of food. This is where observation and common sense are needed. By the time your Rottweiler is two years old, it would be needing only half the protein it required at one year old.

The amount of biscuit meal needed would be approximately the same as the weight of meat per day — slightly less for an eight-week-old puppy, but slightly more by the time it is twelve months old. The important thing is that the puppy

Basic obedience training has already begun for Ravenwood Queen's Request, an English-bred bitch by the imported Thewina Summer Ferrymaster, C.D.X., ex Thewina Stormraven, C.D. Linda Griswold, Indiana, owner.

Feeding

steadily gains weight, and if any bias is found it should be toward the slim side as excess weight can create many problems for a Rottweiler.

An eight-week-old puppy should receive four meals per day (two meat and two milk) and by six months old these can be reduced to three (two meat and one milk). At nine months old the pup can be fed twice per day and it is better that this is then continued throughout its life. Rottweilers are susceptible to bloat and twisted stomachs, and feeding two smaller meals certainly reduces the risk of such problems. In the

Proper diet, exercise, and regular veterinary check-ups and inoculations will ensure that your Rottweiler puppy maintains good health.

foregoing, obviously, as the number of meals per day reduces, the amount per meal increases to give the needed daily ration.

Strong marrow bones are enjoyed by dogs — but chicken and fish bones should be avoided as these could get stuck in the dog's throat — the more so with a Rottweiler's penchant for devouring food as though it were going out of fashion! Some dogs are allergic to cow's milk; goat's milk may prove a good alternative. There are, in fact, few foods a dog will not enjoy, but sweets and "junk foods" are best not given.

45

The breeding of dogs is a complex subject and the detail of pre- and post-natal care of the bitch, together with that of the birth itself and consequential puppy rearing, is beyond the scope of this work. Here we are concerned only with those topics beginners will have to consider before committing themselves to such an undertaking.

BREEDING

There is no justification in allowing any sub-standard animal to breed when there is already in existence a very viable population of that animal. From this it follows that where a Rottweiler has been purchased as a pet, with known failings, it should not be bred from at a later date when the owner has decided that he or she would like to become a breeder. In such cases, they are better advised to retain the pet but purchase another dog more suitable for breeding. This is sound strategy because instead of spending time trying to breed out bad faults, one can concentrate on improving minor matters of type. This will usually result in better puppies which will command higher prices than those resulting from poor-quality parents.

The Bitch

If breeding is planned from the outset, you should purchase the very best female you can afford. It costs no more to feed and keep high-quality stock than to keep inferior animals; possibly less because they will be less likely to develop ailments that are directly attributable to their poor breeding. The novice will not be able to judge what is, and is not, a good brood bitch so this is where, again, it is important to have confidence in the pet shop or breeder you go to. The bitch should have no major failings such as missing or faulty dentition, incorrect ear carriage, or poor general conformation.

For those who might live in more remote areas, or who will be importing from another country, then considerable time should be devoted not only to the quality of the bitch to be acquired but also to the genetic lines of the Rottweilers already in

Unless you are totally committed to the Rottweiler breed—striving to produce dogs with correct structure, type, temperament, and movement—you should not get involved in the breeding of these versatile dogs. Photo by Isabelle Francais.

the area or country. If you are satisfied that there will be suitable studs to put to your bitch, of compatible lines, then you can purchase a puppy; if not, you might need to consider purchasing an in-whelp bitch (which thus means an adult) so as to have the basic building blocks on which to develop your line. This will be a much more expensive proposition.

Should you purchase a puppy for breeding, and should she develop an ailment such as entropion, then I am afraid you must start again. It is quite unethical to breed from stock carrying likely genetic faults that can be "covered up" by surgery. You should report the matter to your national club and seek another bitch; in this way the club can monitor lines with faults, and this can only be to the long-term good of the breed. In any case, you do not want to build on a line you know carries the problem in question.

The Dog (Male)

Obviously, the same criteria applies to the male dog as to the bitch. In fact, it is highly unlikely that a novice would purchase a dog with the initial plan to use it as a stud, simply because its quality needs to be so good. There is no shortage of first class Rottweiler studs, so the only ways in which one can hope to acquire one is to either purchase an existing one, to campaign the dog in the show ring, or to work it in trials or obedience tests. In this way it will prove its worth and owners of bitches will wish to use it. Outstanding stud dogs are rare in any breed, and any top class stud is a valuable animal. In terms of what it can or cannot pass on to its offspring, it has no more value than the bitch, but it has greater importance in that it has far more opportunity to spread its genes than does a female.

Breeding Considerations

Mating a bitch purely on the grounds of low stud fee price, or pure convenience, has nothing to recommend it; a breeder's objective should be to produce successive litters in which the standard of the siblings gets steadily better and is uniform across the litter. To achieve this is very difficult and almost impossible with hit-and-miss strategy based on cost and convenience.

Male Rottweilers are larger, heavier boned, and reflect masculinity in their bearing and expression, while females are smaller and should be distinctly feminine in expression and demeanor. Photo by Isabelle Francais. Owner, Martin Regan.

Snuggling into the whelping box at Delphi Kennels, Florida, is Kismet, a nine-month-old kitten. Al and Bonnie Wimberly, owners.

You must become very aware of the failings in your bitch and then try to select a stud whose genetic lines compliment the female's and who is very strong for the weak points of the bitch. For example, if the bitch has slightly short ears, then you want a dog who has very typically good ears — *not slightly long ones*. The latter is termed compensatory mating. Its problem is that while it may well produce an individual with "perfect" ears, it also increases the chances of others in the litter having ears either overlong or too short. Thus, you have increased the genetic variables for ears in your stock; whereas your objective is to reduce them, that is, make the stock as pure (homozygous) for ear quality as possible.

However, a breeder is not just concerned with good ears as a dog is composed of many, many points; to maintain a high quality in one aspect without losing it on another is what breeding is all about.

Any potential breeder is strongly recommended to purchase a good book on canine breeding and genetics and attempt at least some study on the principles of heredity; without some understanding of the subject, planned breeding is made far more difficult.

Breeding

Matings

By gleaning through breed yearbooks, and by studying the pedigrees of the studs available, you will build up a knowledge of which dogs are prepotent for stamping their type on the breed. Chat to as many other breeders as you can to find out about the short lists of studs you have in mind. The more you know about the stud the better.

Next, you need to check the availability of the stud on the date(s) your bitch will need mating and, indeed, if the dog owner is happy to have his stud cover your bitch. Some very famous Rottweilers were never allowed to mate (or rarely) out-

One of Catherine Thompson's bitches takes a break from maternal duties to get some exercise.

side of their own kennels or lines. It does the reputation of the stud no good at all if it is mated to indifferent bitches just to gain a fee. A litter of poor quality puppies is a very poor advertisement for the dog, even though that quality may have been more the result of the bitch's failings.

If the dog owner is happy for you to use the stud, then you must discuss the terms of the mating. You should have the

agreement in writing. The points will normally comprise:

1. *The Fee*   This is paid at the time of mating but, in the case of an untried male, it may be once the bitch is clearly in whelp or at the birth of the puppies.

2. *Puppy in Lieu of Fee*   Should a puppy (or two) be taken in lieu of a fee, then agreement to cover the eventuality of only one or two puppies surviving should be made (most unlikely in this breed but these things can happen).

3. *Repeat Matings*   These are not obligatory but often agreed to by stud dog owners and will usually take place the next day or the day after.

4. *Choice of Puppy*   If a puppy is to be taken by the stud owner, then is this to be the pick of the litter or the second or third choice? Determine which.

There are no rules whatsoever that govern the terms of a stud dog's use, so it behooves the breeder to clarify these from the outset.

A bitch should not be mated until she is fully mature, usually by 18-24 months (the latter is better). She is most likely to accept the dog between the tenth and fourteenth days. The bitch is normally taken to the dog. Should an extensive journey be needed for you to reach the male, you are advised to have your veterinarian take a vaginal smear from her; from this he can advise the optimum mating day. A successful mating (or tie) will result in puppies 63 days later (but this can vary within a few days). A bitch should not be expected to have puppies in successive seasons. Allow her plenty of time to rebuild her strength before a further litter is permitted.

Should your bitch, by accident, be mated by other than a Rottweiler, consult your vet immediately, within 48 hours of the mating. He can give her a hormonal injection which will nullify the mating and bring her back into season. She should not then be mated until her following season.

Neither dog nor bitch should be used for breeding unless they are in the peak of condition. This is most important for the female who is placed under considerable stress, physically and mentally, in carrying, giving birth, and then rearing the puppies.

Breeding

Time, Space and Cost

Rearing a litter of boisterous Rottweilers is no easy task and is fraught with potential problems. During the first two or three weeks after the birth, the bitch will be doing most of the work, but after this the breeder will find the litter demands more and more time. The pups must be weaned, cleaned, socialized, and attended to when they are ill. As they grow (very quickly!), they will rapidly devour increasing quantities of food, and the money must be there to provide for this. Maybe, if you are lucky, you will find suitable homes for them by the seventh week. But what if you do not? It is essential you consider every negative possibility, one or more of which is sure to become a reality. The prudent breeder lines up homes for each pup before they are born.

From the outset the bitch will need a room to herself, as even a small litter of Rottweilers adds up to a lot of problems if you try to rear them in your kitchen or family room. As they grow they will need plenty of space in which to play, and if they do not all sell, this will also place demands on available space for which you may not have allowed.

Beyond the cost of the stud fee and the food bill, you might have high veterinary fees. The bitch or puppies might be ill; their tails will need docking and there may be vaccinations to pay for. All in all, breeding takes up time, a lot of space, and a whole heap of money. You really should be sure you want to breed Rottweilers before you commit yourself! Seldom do breeders make substantial profits—most are lucky just to break even.

Before bringing a litter of Rottie puppies into this world, make certain that you have good homes lined up for them.

T he dog show is the shop window for those who breed dogs. This is the way in which they find out how well their stock compares with that of other breeders. You do not have to be a breeder to compete in shows, but obviously it is an on-going situation as the show life of a dog is restricted to

EXHIBITING

but a few years. There are many levels of shows ranging from informal local ones, through those restricted to a single breed (specialty shows) to the large multi-breed spectaculars, of which Crufts and Westminster are probably the most famous.

Any potential exhibitor is advised to attend a few shows, of differing size, in order to become familiar with procedures and to see the standard of the competition. You should become *au fait* with the standard of your country and of the rules that govern exhibition, which vary from one nation to another. Both of these requirements can be obtained from your national kennel club and are usually supplied at no cost. It may even be possible that your line of dogs may be better sold in another country because of that country's standard for the breed.

If you intend to exhibit your dog, plan its career well in advance. Although many people exhibit Rottweilers at very young ages, this is not really recommended in such a slow maturing breed, as often such dogs "go over" very quickly and have short show lives. Serious competition against fully matured, quality Rottweilers should not be attempted until your dog is about 18 months old. Prior to this, your goal is to prepare your dog, physically and mentally, to what lies ahead. All too often one sees young dogs being rushed around the country and thrust into show after show before the dog has even been

If you plan to show your Rottweiler, become well acquainted with the breed standard of perfection, which describes what the ideal Rottweiler should look like and how it should behave.

allowed to be a puppy. Both owner and dog should enjoy the occasion, but if you become consumed by the desire to be a winner at any cost, then this is unlikely ever to be the case.

One sees those owners who show their obvious dislike of any judge who places them well down the line. Worse, they then exhibit their obvious annoyance by being short-tempered with their dogs — whom they promptly place on their bench before retiring to the bar in order to inform those who will listen just how little the judge knows about Rottweilers. It's the same in all breeds, and this sort of exhibitor the show world can do without! Dog showing is a sport, but one has to say that at the major events commercial aspects have become a prime motivation for winning.

The Exhibition Dog

In order to succeed in the show-ring it is important that your dog does not lose out purely because your competitors have prepared their dogs better for exhibition. Clearly, each dog must be in superb physical condition and have been groomed regularly. Then there is the temperamental aspect. The dog must be prepared to let the judge inspect its mouth, feel its muscle, and view it from behind (some dogs can get very annoyed if people stand right behind them). You must be able to stand the dog in such a way ("stack" it) as to show off its virtues while not highlighting minor flaws. It is the judge's job to evaluate these flaws as well as the merits. If you enter a major show thinking it's all up to the dog, you will soon be disillusioned. For this reason there are many professional handlers in Rottweilers, and many highly skilled breeders as well, who know just how best to present and exhibit. Start your dog off at the smaller events where both you and your dog can begin to gain experience.

Ringcraft Classes

In order to perfect your show technique, and to accustom your Rottweiler to the show world, the joining of a local club which has ringcraft classes is recommended. It is even better if the instructor is familiar with this breed. You will be advised when you and your dog have reached a reasonable stan-

Bred by Virginia Aceti and Sheryl Hedrick of Pioneer Kennels, Champion Brash Baer von Pioneer, C.D., and Champion Pioneer's Brute Force, C.D., are one of the few Rottweiler Braces to have won Best Brace in Show. Ted and Kandy Galotti and Sheryl Hedrick, co-owners.

dard and can then map out the various shows in which you wish to compete. These should be on a build-up basis over 18 months so the dog has plenty of time to mature and gain experience, but where the atmosphere is less charged. Some exhibitors never make the top honors but still derive great pleasure from competing at the lesser shows, simply for the friends they make and the enjoyment of a day out.

Champions

Everyone would like to make his dog a champion Rottweiler; to achieve this distinction in the USA, Canada, and Australia, one has to acquire a number of points, including some which are termed *majors*. In the UK one has to win three challenge certificates, under three different judges. In my opinion, it is probably harder to reach   championship in the UK than in most other countries, as one will be continually coming up against the leading champions of the day. This means that many fine dogs, which make their championships in other countries, are denied. However, it can also result in a dog's being over-rated purely because it became a champion. Each system has its merits and negatives.

Obedience, Agility, and Working Trials

For those who really want to test both their own and their dog's abilities to the limit, the answer must be one of the obedience-based aspects of Rottweiler owning. The Rottweiler is a working breed and while normal show-ring work is fine, it does not in any way test *ability*, only *beauty*. The two are not always complimentary with each other.

Both obedience and agility tests are run in conjunction with major dog shows but Working Trials are a totally separate entity. Rottweilers are very competent at obedience work (heel, sit, stay, recall, scent discrimination) but one has to say that they seem to find it all a bit mundane after a while so are never as successful at it as are Border Collies or German Shepherd Dogs, for example—both breeds which have long track records for this type of work. Likewise, agility tests do not favor a heavy breed like the Rottweiler which was never intended to be a speedy, nimble breed. These latter competitions have become very popular, as the dogs compete over an obstacle course and can be very amusing as well as interesting for the spectators. Dogs seem to enjoy them and the crowds watching can get very excited when it is run against the clock.

Working trials test the dog to its limit over all types of terrain and in all weathers. There are numerous qualifications that can be gained as the dog proceeds toward the title of Working Trial Champion, the ultimate accolade. All forms of obedience require considerable patience on the part of the owner, but there is a very special feeling of achievement, and a bond between dog and owner, as success is achieved and a task well performed.

OFFICIAL STANDARD

The Board of Directors of the American Kennel Club has approved the following revised Standard for Rottweilers:
• ***General Appearance***—*The ideal Rottweiler is a large, robust and powerful dog, black with clearly defined rust markings. His compact build denotes great strength, agility and endurance. Males are characteristically larger, heavier boned and more masculine in appearance.*

A six-foot lead is a useful piece of equipment to have on hand when teaching your Rottweiler such basic obedience commands as "sit," "stay," "heel," "come," and "down." Photo by Ron Reagan. Breeder/owner, Ron Gibson.

- **Size**—Males, 24" to 27"; Females, 22" to 25". Proportion should always be considered rather than height alone. The length of the body from the breast bone (sternum) to the rear edge of the pelvis (ischium) is slightly longer than the height of the dog at the withers, the most desirable proportion being as 10 is to 9. Depth of chest should be fifty percent of the height. SERIOUS FAULTS—Lack of proportion, undersize, oversize.

- **Head**—Of medium length, broad between the ears; forehead line seen in profile is moderately arched. Cheekbones and stop well developed; length of muzzle should not exceed distance between stop and occiput. Skull is preferred dry, however some wrinkling may occur when dog is alert.

- **Muzzle**—Bridge is straight, broad at base with slight tapering towards tip. Nose is broad rather than round, with black nostrils.

- **Lips**—Always black; corners tightly closed. Inner mouth pigment is dark. A pink mouth is to be penalized.

- **Teeth**—42 in number (20 upper and 22 lower); strong, correctly placed, meeting in a scissors bite—lower incisors touching inside of upper incisors. SERIOUS FAULTS: Any missing tooth, level bite. DISQUALIFICATIONS: Undershot, overshot, four or more missing teeth.

- **Eyes**—Of medium size, moderately deep set, almond shaped with well-fitting lids. Iris of uniform color, from medium to dark brown—the darker shade is always preferred. SERIOUS FAULTS: Yellow (bird of prey) eyes; eyes not of same color; eyes unequal in size or shape. Hairless lid.

- **Ears**—Pendant, proportionately small, triangular in shape; set well apart and placed on skull so as to make it appear broader when the dog is alert. Ear terminates at approximate mid-cheek level. Correctly held, the inner edge will lie tightly against cheek.

- **Neck**—Powerful, well muscled, moderately long with slight arch and without loose skin.

- **Body**—Topline is firm and level, extending in straight line from withers to croup.

- **Brisket**—Deep, reaching to elbow.

- **Chest**—Roomy, broad with well-pronounced forechest.

- **Ribs**—Well sprung.

- **Loin**—*Short, deep and well muscled.*
- **Croup**—*Broad, medium length, slightly sloping.*
- **Tail**—*Normally carried in horizontal position—giving impression of an elongation of top line. Carried slightly above horizontal when dog is excited. Some dogs are born without a tail, or a very short stub. Tail is normally docked short close to the body. The set of the tail is more important than length.*
- **Forequarters**—SHOULDER BLADE—*Long, well laid back at 45 degree angle. Elbows tight, well under body. Distance from withers to elbow and elbow to ground is equal.*

LEGS—*Strongly developed with straight, heavy bone. Not set closely together.* PASTERNS—*Strong, springy and almost perpendicular to ground.* FEET—*Round, compact, well arched toes, turning neither in nor out. Pads thick and hard; nails short, strong and black. Dewclaws may be removed.*

- **Hindquarters**—*Angulation of hindquarters balances that of forequarters.* UPPER THIGH—*Fairly long, braod and well muscled.* STIFLE JOINT—*Moderately angulated.* LOWER THIGH—*Long, powerful, extensively muscled leading into a strong hock joint; metatarsus nearly perpendicular to ground. Viewed from rear, hind legs are straight and wide enough apart to fit in with a properly built body.* FEET—*Somewhat longer than front feet, well arched toes turning neither in nor out. Dewclaws must be removed if present.*
- **Coat**—*Outer coat is straight, coarse, dense, medium length, lying flat. Undercoat must be present on neck and thighs, but should not show through the outer coat. The Rottweiler should be exhibited in a natural condition without trimming, except to remove whiskers, if desired.* FAULT—*Wavy coat.* SERIOUS FAULTS—*Excessively short coat, curly or open coat, lack of undercoat.* DISQUALIFICATION—*Long coat.*
- **Color**—*Always black with rust to mahogany markings. The borderline between black and rust should be clearly defined. The markings should be located as follows: a spot over each eye; on cheeks, as a strip around each side of the muzzle, but not on the bridge of nose; on throat; triangular mark on either side of breastbone; on forelegs from carpus downward to toes; on inside of rear legs showing down the front of stifle and broadening out to front of rear legs from hock to toes; but not*

completely eliminating black from back of legs; under tail. Black penciling markings on toes. The undercoat is gray or black. Quantity and location of rust markings is important and should not exceed ten percent of body color. Insufficient or excessive markings should be penalized. SERIOUS FAULTS—*Excessive markings; white markings any place on dog (a few white hairs do not constitute a marking); light-colored markings.* DISQUALIFICATIONS: *Any base color other than black; total absence of markings.*

• **Gait**—*The Rottweiler is a trotter. The motion is harmonious, sure, powerful and unhindered, with a strong fore-reach and a powerful rear drive. Front and rear legs are thrown neither in nor out, as the imprint of hind feet should touch that of forefeet. In a trot, the forequarters and hindquarters are mutually co-ordinated while the back remains firm; as speed is increased legs will converge under body towards a center line.*

• **Character**—*The Rottweiler should possess a fearless expression with a self-assured aloofness that does not lend itself to immediate and indiscriminate friendships. He has an inherent desire to protect home and family and is an intelligent dog of extreme hardness and adaptability with a strong willingness to work. A judge shall dismiss from the ring any shy or vicious Rottweiler.*

• **Shyness**—*A dog shall be judged fundamentally shy if, refusing to stand for examination, it shrinks away from the judge; if it fears an approach from the rear; if it shies at sudden or unusual noises to a marked degree.*

• **Viciousness**—*A dog that attacks or attempts to attack either the judge or its handler is definitely vicious. An aggressive or belligerent attitude towards other dogs shall not be deemed viciousness.*

• **Faults**—*The foregoing is a description of the ideal Rottweiler. Any structural fault that detracts from the above-described working dog must be penalized to the extent of the deviation.*

• **Disqualifications**—*Undershot, overshot, four or more missing teeth. Long coat, Any base color other than black; total absence of markings.*

Suggested Reading

HOW TO SHOW YOUR OWN DOG
By Virginia Tuck Nichols
ISBN 0-87666-661-6
PS-607

You don't necessarily need a professional handler to show your dog. What you do need is some basic information about dog shows, how a champion is made, what the terms and definitions are, and how to prepare for the big day.
Hard cover, 5½" x 8½", 288 pages 136 black and white photos; 10 line illustrations.

DOGS FOR PROTECTION
By Lucine H. Flynn
ISBN 0-87666-813-9
PS-802

This book contains detailed information about choosing a dog to provide protection and about training dogs in the basic obedience routines that every protection dog must know. The author, a recognized expert in obedience teaching and judging, outlines step-by-step exercises for training a dog to be protective and alert, but not a snarling beast. This is a very practical volume.
Hard cover, 5½" x 8", 96 pages 41 full-color photos, 29 black and white photos.

DOG OWNER'S VETERINARY GUIDE
By G. W. Stamm
ISBN 0-87666-402-8
AP-927

The most accurate and up-to-date book based on recent information set forth by various notable veterinarians.
Hard cover, 5½" x 8", 112 pages 28 black and white photos, 39 line drawings.

DOG BREEDING FOR PROFESSIONALS
By Dr. Herbert Richards
ISBN 0-87666-659-4
H-969

For dog owners who need and actively seek advice about how to go about breeding their dogs either for profit or purely because of their attachment to their animals. *Please note:* This book contains highly explicit photos of canine sexual activities that some readers may find offensive.
Hard cover, 5½" x 8½", 224 pages 105 black and white photos, 62 full-color photos, 4 charts.

DOG TRAINING
By Lew Burke
ISBN 0-87666-656-X
H-962

The elements of dog training are easy to grasp and apply, and this guide is for dog owners age 14 and older who are anxious to discover the secrets behind Lew Burke's methods.
Hard cover, 5½" x 8½", 255 pages 64 black and white photos, 23 full-color photos.

Index